MILITARY DRONES

by Matt Chandler

Consultant:
Raymond L. Puffer, PhD
Historian, Retired
Edwards Air Force Base History Office

CAPSTONE PRESS
a capstone imprint

T0081147

Edge Books are published by Capstone Press,
1710 Roe Crest Drive, North Mankato, Minnesota 56003
www.mycapstone.com

Library of Congress Cataloging-in-Publication Data
Names: Chandler, Matt, author.
Title: Military drones / by Matt Chandler.
Description: North Mankato, Minnesota : Capstone Press, [2017] | Series: Edge books.
Drones. | Includes bibliographical references and index. | Audience: Age 8-14. | Audience:
Grade 4 to 6.
Identifiers: LCCN 2016023854| ISBN 9781515737698 (library binding) | ISBN
9781515737773 (pbk.) | ISBN 9781515737971 (ebook (pdf))
Subjects: LCSH: Uninhabited combat aerial vehicles--United States--Juvenile literature. |
Drone aircraft--United States--Juvenile literature.
Classification: LCC UG1242.D7 C44 2017 | DDC 623.74/69--dc23
LC record available at https://lccn.loc.gov/2016023854

Editorial Credits
Carrie Sheely, editor; Steve Mead, designer; Tracey Engel, media researcher;
Katy LaVigne, production specialist

Photo Credits
Air National Guard Photo: 20-21; AP Photo: 24-25; BAE Systems: 9; Getty Images: Ed
Darack, 23, Florilegius/SSPL, 7, Nigel Roddis, 19; Lockheed Martin Aeronautics Company:
26-27; NASA Langley: David C. Bowman, 28-29; Newscom: NEIL HALL/REUTERS, 11; Photo
by Staff Sgt. Samuel Morse, 16-17; Shutterstock: Andis Rea, Design Element, boscorelli, Front
and Back Cover, Brothers Good, Cover and Interior Design Element, DamienGeso, Design
Element, Kolonko, Design Element, Konstantin Ustinov, Design Element, Nik Merkulov, Cover
and Interior Design Element, Pagina, Design Element, Pisit Rapitpunt, Cover Background,
robuart, Design Element, slavapolo, Design Element, tratong, Design Element, Vjom, Cover
and Interior Design Element; U.S. Air Force Photo: Lt. Col. Leslie Pratt, 4-5, Paul Ridgeway,
14-15, Senior Airman Cory D. Payne, 8, Mass Communication Specialist 1st Class Keith E.
Jones/Released, 12

Printed and bound in the USA.
052018 000482

TABLE OF CONTENTS

CHAPTER 1

A SNEAK ATTACK

It's November 2007. The United States is leading a **coalition** of armed forces in the Iraq War (2003–2011). U.S. soldiers are advancing in the town of Balad. Balad has been a hotspot in the war, and the soldiers are in incredible danger. Three Iraqi **insurgents** fire **mortars** at the troops.

coalition—an alliance of people, groups, or countries working together toward a common goal

insurgent—a person who rebels and fights against his or her country's ruling government and those supporting it

mortar—a short cannon that fires shells or rockets high in the air

The insurgents are focused on the ground troops. They have no idea that an MQ-1 Predator drone is above them. The operator of this 27-foot- (8.2-meter-) long unmanned aerial vehicle (UAV) is about to take action. The Predator fires a single air-to-ground missile, killing the Iraqi insurgents and saving the American soldiers.

Military drones are a sign that modern warfare is changing. In the sky and underwater, military drones complete thousands of missions each year. With each mission, the drones have the potential to save lives.

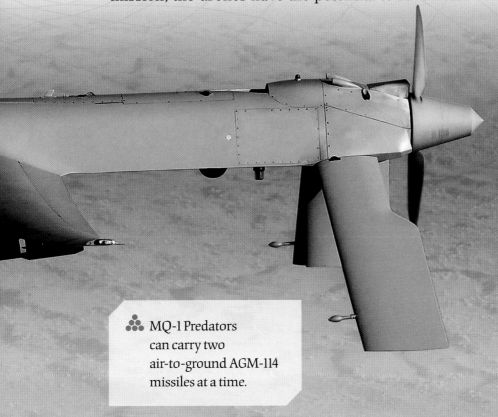

MQ-1 Predators can carry two air-to-ground AGM-114 missiles at a time.

CHAPTER 2

HISTORY OF MILITARY DRONES

What is a drone? The answer has changed over time. Generally, drones are unmanned vehicles that operate by **remote control**. Most people think of drones as aircraft, but they also travel in water. Drones come in many shapes and sizes and have different purposes. Military drones can be traced back more than 160 years. In 1849 Austria launched an attack on Venice, Italy, using unmanned balloons fitted with bombs.

Since Austria's balloon attacks, certain inventions helped advance military drones. In 1898 inventor Nikola Tesla figured out a way to control a vehicle using remote control. Tesla's invention eventually caught on. It allowed unmanned aircraft to be directed with greater accuracy than ever before.

 remote control—a device used to control machines from a distance

Near the end of World War I (1914–1918), the
Dayton-Wright Airplane Company developed the
Kettering Bug. It was one of the first drones to look like
a plane. Built for the U.S. Army, it had a wingspan of
nearly 15 feet (4.6 meters). The drone carried a large
bomb. After launching, the engine would run for a preset
number of **revolutions**. Then the drone would simply fall
out of the sky toward its target. However, the war ended
before Kettering Bugs could be used in combat.

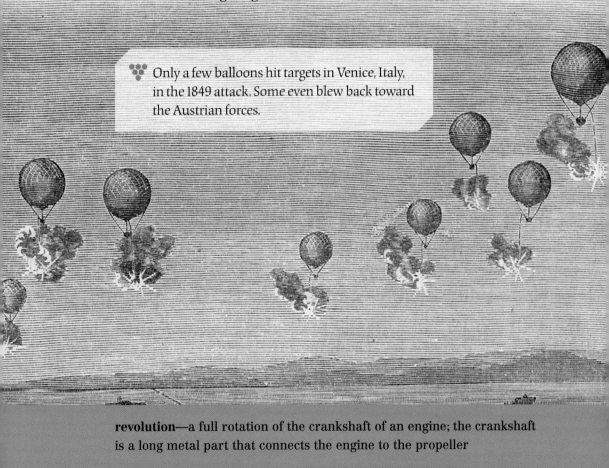

Only a few balloons hit targets in Venice, Italy,
in the 1849 attack. Some even blew back toward
the Austrian forces.

revolution—a full rotation of the crankshaft of an engine; the crankshaft
is a long metal part that connects the engine to the propeller

The MQ-9 Reaper can carry more weapons and equipment than the Predator.

DRONE ADVANCEMENT

1849

Austria launches an unmanned balloon attack on Italy. Some of the bombs explode as planned. Others blow off course

1898

Nikola Tesla shows how his remote control boat works in Madison Square Garden, New York.

1945

During World War II (1939–1945), Japan launches pilotless balloons armed with bombs in an attack on the United

1970s and 1980s

With computer and navigational technology advances in place, military drones begin to look and act

1995

The **Global Positioning System** (GPS) becomes fully operational; the United States puts the Predator drone into service.

In 1935 Great Britain's Royal Navy designed Queen Bees. These drones could fly more than 100 miles (161 kilometers) per hour. The Royal Navy used the drones for target practice.

The biggest technology breakthrough came with the U.S. Air Force Predator drone. Aircraft manufacturer Lockheed Martin built the **reconnaissance** drone in the mid-1990s. In 2001 the Predator was modified to deliver missiles and other weapons. The United States used the Predator model to build other UAVs.

reconnaissance—a mission to gather information about an enemy

Global Positioning System—an electronic tool used to find the location of an object; this system uses signals from satellites

THROUGH THE YEARS

2001

On September 11 terrorists attack the United States. Afterward, the United States uses Predators extensively in the wars in Iraq and Afghanistan.

2007

The United States puts the MQ-9 Reaper into service. This drone is similar to the Predator, but it flies farther and faster.

2013

Great Britain's Taranis makes its first flight. The Unmanned Combat Air System demonstrator has completed several flight

2015

The U.S. Navy launches a drone from a submarine for the first time.

2016

The British government purchases two Zephyr-8 drones. The drones are unique because they are solar powered. The

CHAPTER 3

DRONES FOR ALL KINDS OF JOBS

Modern military drones can look very different from one another. Some UAVs look like helicopters, while others look like airplanes. Most unmanned underwater vehicles (UUVs) are shaped like submarines. But no matter how they appear, all drones can detect and send information.

Imagine a drone so small it fits in the palm of your hand. The Black Hornet UAV does just that. A soldier simply tosses it into the air to launch it. An operator flies the drone with a small handheld controller. Black Hornets can fly for 20 minutes at a time. They can see what is over a wall or around a corner. The drones send images or live video back to the operators for viewing on a screen.

The Black Hornet's frame is made of strong plastic.

CLOSE UP

FACT

The Black Hornet drone was originally designed to appear more like a flying insect than a war drone.

The U.S. Navy has increased its use of underwater drones in recent years. Among the U.S. Navy's drone fleet is the REMUS 600. The 10-foot- (3-meter-) long tube-shaped drone collects valuable information underwater. It has **sonar** and a GPS to help with **navigation**. The Navy uses the drone to search for deadly mines on the ocean floor and for reconnaissance.

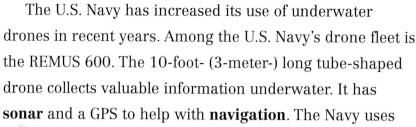

A Navy sailor retrieves a REMUS 600 after testing near Hawaii.

sonar—a device that uses sound waves to find underwater objects; sonar stands for sound navigation and ranging

navigation—using instruments and charts to find your way in a ship or other vehicle

DRONES AROUND THE WORLD

More than 100 military drones are in use today.
Here are just a few operating around the world.

MQ-1 PREDATOR

INTRODUCED: **1994 (weaponized 2001)**

PRIMARY USES: **reconnaissance, weapon strikes**

IN USE BY: **United States, Italy, Morocco, Turkey, United Arab Emirates, Others**

* Some of these are unarmed models designed for international sale called Predator XPs.

MQ-9 REAPER

INTRODUCED: **2007**

PRIMARY USES: **reconnaissance, weapon strikes**

IN USE BY: **United States, Great Britain, Italy, France, Spain, Others**

RQ-4 GLOBAL HAWK

INTRODUCED: **1998**

PRIMARY USES: **surveillance**

IN USE BY: **United States (military and NASA)**

CAIHONG 5

INTRODUCED: **2015**

PRIMARY USES: **combat**

IN USE BY: **China**

HERON

INTRODUCED: **1994**

PRIMARY USES: **reconnaissance**

IN USE BY: **Israel, Brazil, Turkey, India**

WATCHKEEPER WK-450

INTRODUCED: **2014**

PRIMARY USES: **reconnaissance, surveillance**

IN USE BY: **Great Britain**

EADS BARRACUDA

INTRODUCED: **2006 (demonstrator model only)**

PRIMARY USES: **reconnaissance, combat**

IN USE BY: **Spain, Germany**

SWORDFISH

INTRODUCED: **2008**

PRIMARY USES: **search and mapping in shallow water**

IN USE BY: **United States**

CHAPTER 4

INSIDE A MILITARY DRONE

Militaries are just one type of drone user. In recent years the use of drones for business and recreation has increased greatly. Hundreds of thousands of recreational drones operate in the United States alone. So what sets military drones apart? What amazing technology is packed into one of these machines?

Take a look at the MQ-9 Reaper. It has a complex communications and sensor system. One device can link to a suspected terrorist's phone using the phone's SIM card. Once linked, the Predator can more easily track the terrorist. A Ground Moving Target Indicator (GMTI) helps the Reaper track moving vehicles on the ground.

An MQ-9 Reaper can carry a variety of weapons under its body.

HOW MQ-9 REAPER WEAPONRY WORKS

The ability to carry weapons is one of the biggest differences between military and nonmilitary drones. The MQ-9 Reaper can carry a combination of laser-guided bombs, satellite-guided bombs, air-to-air missiles, and AGM-114 "Hellfire" missiles. Its weapons are capable of destroying entire military installations.

AGM-114 "Hellfire" missiles:
Lasers guide these powerful air-to-ground missiles.

AIM-9 Sidewinder air-to-air missiles:
These missiles sense heat from the exhaust of an enemy aircraft. The missiles move toward the heat.

GBU-12 laser-guided bombs:
A laser is aimed at a target to mark it. The bombs launch, and the onboard computer guides the bombs to their marked targets.

GBU-38 satellite-guided bombs:
A GPS guides these bombs toward their targets.

Impressed with a smartphone's photos? You probably wouldn't be if you saw a photo from an advanced military drone! Many recreational drones can take professional-quality videos and photographs from 400 feet (122 m) in the air. But a Predator surveillance drone is said to be capable of reading a license plate from 2 miles (3.2 km) away! A combination of cameras are fitted on an MQ-1 Predator. Operators use video from the full-color camera to fly the drone. An **infrared** camera helps it "see" at night and in low light conditions.

FACT

A very fast recreational drone travels 60 miles (97 km) per hour. In comparison, the MQ-9 Reaper can reach a top speed of about 275 miles (443 km) per hour.

 nose cameras of an MQ-1 Predator

infrared—a type of light that is invisible to human eyes

CHAPTER 5

MILITARY DRONES AT WORK

The media regularly talked about the number of ground troops fighting during the height of the Iraq War. But some military pilots fought in the war without ever leaving their base. U.S. Air Force airmen operated most drones in Iraq from Nevada.

Predator and Reaper operators fly drones much like how people play video games. They operate a series of controls and watch the action live on a bank of monitors in front of them. But this isn't a video game. Lives hang in the balance. From more than 7,000 miles (11,265 km) away, they can fire a missile from their drone to kill enemies.

FACT

The increased usage of military drones led to a shortage of U.S. drone pilots in 2015. The lack of operators led to a reduction in drone missions. The Air Force plans to add pilots and the number of bases that operate drones to keep up with demand.

A traditional military plane usually has just two pilots. But Predators and Reapers may need as many as 15 operators for a mission. Predators and Reapers can stay airborne for more than 24 hours. Three crews may have to work in rotation to complete a flight.

Drone operators from the Royal Air Force control drones flying in Afghanistan from a ground control station in Waddington, England.

DRONES IN TIMES OF PEACE

Military drones travel to dangerous combat zones to collect information and conduct attacks. But how are these drones used in times of peace? What role do drones play when there isn't an enemy to hunt?

In Europe military drone manufacturer Schiebel partnered with a humanitarian organization to use drones. The organization's mission was to help locate refugees in the Mediterranean Sea. The drones were able to find people at night using infrared equipment.

In the United States, the military has used drones to assist after natural disasters. In 2013 the California Air National Guard used its MQ-1 Predator to assist with an out-of-control wildfire. The blaze had already burned more than 160,000 acres (64,750 hectares). Nearly 4,000 firefighters were trying to control it. The National Guard used the Predator to map out the areas in need of support and track where the fire was spreading.

The Air National Guard has also used drones to search for missing people. In the summer of 2015, a man was reported missing in California's huge El Dorado National Forest. The Guard launched an MQ-9 Reaper to help search for him. The drone was equipped with a **thermal** imaging camera that can detect heat. Sadly, the man had died before he was found. But the use of a drone to search for a missing person was unique.

The California Air National Guard's 2015 search was the first time its Reaper was involved in a search and rescue mission.

thermal—having to do with heat; thermal cameras can detect heat

CHAPTER 6

MILITARY DRONE DEBATES

Many people have spoken out against the use of drones in wartime. Some experts say military drone use increases the number of innocent civilians that are killed.

The U.S. military has launched hundreds of drone attacks in the Middle East. Most are kept highly secret. But the government has acknowledged that hundreds and maybe thousands of civilians have been killed in drone attacks. Among those killed by U.S. drone strikes were one American hostage and one Italian hostage. These hostages were being held by the terrorist group al-Qaeda in 2015. As of April 2015, at least eight Americans have been killed in overseas drone strikes.

FACT

In 2000 the U.S. Pentagon oversaw a fleet of less than 50 drones. By 2010 that number grew to about 7,500.

But people in favor of expanded drone use point out that drones save many lives. Soldiers can launch small drones such as Black Hornets to look ahead and spot enemies, roadside bombs, or other dangers. Having these drones in the field reduces the risk of soldiers being ambushed and killed.

A U.S. Marine launches a UAV in Afghanistan.

OTHER RISKS OF DRONES

The Reaper weighs almost 2.5 tons (2.3 metric tons). Drone crashes endanger innocent lives on the ground. If a Reaper hits a public building or gathering place, the **casualties** could be huge. In 2015 the U.S. Air Force lost 20 Reapers that crashed in countries around the world. Very little is known about these crashes because most details are **classified** by the U.S. military. A 2013 report found that 450 British military drones crashed over a five-year period. Among the lost drones was a Reaper equipped with Hellfire missiles that cost more than $14 million.

U.S. military experts examine the remains of a Predator that crashed in Turkey in 2016.

SECRET TECHNOLOGY AT RISK

Besides causing injuries, other risks are involved when drones crash in enemy territory. Many countries will examine a downed drone and try to **replicate** the technology to build their own drones. There is also the risk that enemy forces can retrieve the video and other data from the drone to use against its enemies.

casualty—a person injured or killed in an accident or a war

classified—top secret

replicate—to repeat or copy something exactly

CHAPTER 7

THE DRONES OF TOMORROW

The technology behind military drones is constantly changing. The original Predator drone flew just 84 miles (134 km) per hour. This made it an easy target to shoot down. Compare that to a new drone concept that Lockheed Martin is reportedly developing. Named the SR-72, developers estimate the spy and attack drone will be able to travel more than 4,000 miles (6,437 km) per hour! That's six times the speed of sound. The SR-72 is expected to be ready to fly missions by 2030.

Imagine that a terror suspect is on the loose in London. The British military is looking for him. How might they find him? There are millions of ways to blend in to crowds. Research teams have outfitted some drones with special facial recognition software. Someday militaries may be able to load pictures of a suspected terrorist into a drone's computer. The drone would then scan every face it "sees" and look for matches. This use of drone technology could save countless lives.

The SR-72's design and high speeds would make it difficult for enemies to detect.

LIMITLESS POSSIBILITIES

Faster, more advanced drones will be able to do much more than today's military drones. In 2011 the U.S. Navy unveiled its X-47B drone **prototype**. It is the first unmanned aircraft that can take off from an aircraft carrier and return. Someday fighter pilots may remain safe while advanced drones launch from aircraft carriers in their place.

NASA's GL-10 is impressive for a different reason. It can take off like a helicopter, rising vertically into the air. But once it's airborne, the GL-10 flies like an airplane! This advance in technology may allow drones to operate in areas where there is no room for a runway-style takeoff.

FACT

China is developing **stealth** drones such as the futuristic Sharp Sword. These drones would be very difficult for radar defense systems to detect.

prototype—the first version of an invention that tests an idea to see if it will work

stealth—the ability to move secretly

From the sea and air, military drones have changed the way militaries fight wars. As drones become more advanced, military forces will find even more ways to use these amazing machines.

NASA's GL-10 prototype has eight motors on the wings and two motors on its tail.

GLOSSARY

casualty (KAZH-oo-uhl-tee)—a person injured or killed in an accident or a war

classified (KLAH-suh-fide)—top secret

coalition (ko-a-LI-shuhn)—an alliance of people, groups, or countries working together toward a common goal

Global Positioning System (GLOH-buhl puh-ZI-shuhn-ing SISS-tuhm)—an electronic tool used to find the location of an object; this system uses signals from satellites

infrared (in-fruh-RED)—a type of light that is invisible to human eyes

insurgent (in-SUR-juhnt)—a person who rebels and fights against his or her country's ruling government and those supporting it

mortar (MOR-tur)—a short cannon that fires shells or rockets high in the air

navigation (NAV-uh-gay-shuhn)—using instruments and charts to find your way in a ship or other vehicle

prototype (PROH-tuh-tipe)—the first version of an invention that tests an idea to see if it will work

reconnaissance (ree-KAH-nuh-suhnss)—a mission to gather information about an enemy

remote control (ri-MOHT kuhn-TROHL)—a device used to control machines from a distance

replicate (re-PLI-kayt)—to repeat or copy something exactly

revolution (rev-oh-LOO-shuhn)—a full rotation of the crankshaft of an engine; the crankshaft is a long metal part that connects the engine to the propeller

sonar (SOH-nar)—a device that uses sound waves to find underwater objects; sonar stands for sound navigation and ranging

stealth (STELTH)—the ability to move secretly

thermal (THUR-muhl)—having to do with heat; thermal cameras can detect heat

READ MORE

Collard, Sneed. *Technology Forces: Drones and War Machines.* New York: Rourke Educational Media, 2013.

Faust, Daniel. *Drones: Eyes in the Skies.* New York: PowerKids Press, 2016.

Scholastic. *Drones: From Insect Spy Drones to Bomber Drones.* New York: Scholastic, 2014.

INTERNET SITES

FactHound offers a safe, fun way to find Internet sites related to this book. All of the sites on FactHound have been researched by our staff.
Here's all you do:

Visit *www.facthound.com*

Type in this code: 9781515737698

 Check out projects, games and lots more at **www.capstonekids.com**

INDEX